DID ANYTHING GOOD COME OUT OF...

WORLD WAR TWO?

EMMA MARRIOTT

Published in Great Britain in 2017 by Wayland

Produced for Wayland by Tall Tree Ltd
Designers: Jonathan Vipond and Ed Simkins
Editors: Jon Richards and Joe Fullman

Dewey number: 940.5'3-dc23
ISBN 978 0 7502 9729 5

FSC

Wayland, an imprint of Hachette Children's Group
Part of Hodder and Stoughton
Carmelite House
50 Victoria Embankment
London EC4Y 0DZ

An Hachette UK Company
www.hachette.co.uk
www.hachettechildrens.co.uk

Printed and bound in China

10 9 8 7 6 5 4 3 2 1

The publisher would like to thank the following for their kind permission to reproduce their photographs:

Key: (t) top; (c) centre; (b) bottom; (l) left; (r) right

The following images are public domain: Front Cover br, Back Cover cl, cbl.
4bl, 5tr bl, 6–7c, 7cr, 8cr b, 9tr c, 10bl, 11tr br, 13tr, 14tr bl, 15cr, 16b, 18c bl, 19tr cr, 22cl br,
22–23tc, 23br, 24tl bl, 25tl cl br bl, 26tl, 27tl cl, 28bl, 28tr, 32tl, 34–35t, 37tr, 38t br, 40t br,
41cl tr cr br, 42–43c, 43cl, 44tl, 47br.

All other images istock.com unless otherwise indicated.

Front Cover tr NASA. Back Cover tl German Federal Archive.
6tl German Federal Archive, 5br German Federal Archive, 7bl German Federal Archive, 10br Antonov14,
15tl Shutterstock.com, 15bl Russian International News Agency/Max Alpert, 17b George Louis,
21br Christophe Marcheux, 23tr German Federal Archive, 28t German Federal Archive, 28bc RadioFan,
29b Draco2008, 32br Otis Historical Archives of National Museum of Health & Medicine, 33b Wellcome Trust,
39tr Moviestore collection Ltd/Alamy, 39br AF archive/Alamy, 40cl German Federal Archive,
41tl German Federal Archive, 44cl Ted Coles.
Every attempt has been made to clear copyright. Should there be any inadvertent omission,
please apply to the publisher for rectification.

CONTENTS

COMBAT IN THE SKIES

Between July and October 1940, the Royal Air Force and German Luftwaffe battled it out in the skies during the Battle of Britain. Young pilots on both sides found themselves on the front line as the Germans launched a large and sustained bombing campaign against Britain in preparation for a full-scale invasion.

British Spitfire and Hurricane aircraft take part in an aerial dog fight against a German Messerschmitt during the Battle of Britain.

THE BATTLE OF BRITAIN

Air combat during the Battle of Britain could be bewildering and intense, and pilots on both sides demonstrated tremendous bravery and skill. Britain, however, had both the most advanced radar early warning system in the world and the most effective interceptor fighter plane, the Spitfire, enabling it to triumph. The British lost more than 900 aircraft but shot down 1,700 German planes. As a result, in October 1940, Hitler put aside his plans to invade Britain, a major turning point in World War II.

"I GOT TWO OF THEM BY SHEER FLUKE, SHUTTING MY EYES... I WAS JUST SPRAYING THEM HOPING FOR THE BEST AND TRYING TO GET OUT OF THE WAY."

George Unwin, an RAF Spitfire pilot, unexpectedly flies into a German escort of Messerschmitt fighter planes during the Battle of Britain.

1933
The Nazi Party wins the German election and Hitler is appointed Chancellor.

1935
Hitler orders Germany to re-arm and re-introduces military conscription, both banned by the Versailles Treaty.

1936
Hitler joins the Fascist Italian leader Mussolini in an alliance known as the Rome-Berlin Axis.

LIGHTNING WAR

The Battle of Britain marked the first major battle fought in the air, and showed the increasingly important role of technology, aircraft and modern weapons in warfare. Hitler's fast-moving tanks and blitzkrieg ('lightning war') tactics enabled Germany to overrun countries rapidly. Military combat on land, in the air and at sea, the bombing of cities and genocide conducted on an enormous scale would lead to some 50 million deaths across the globe, most of them civilian.

HOW CAN ANYTHING GOOD COME OUT OF A WAR?

Did this terror and destruction act as a trigger for change? Did it bring an end to conflict and better cooperation between nations? Did it lead to social reforms, or spur on scientific and technological innovation? Was this a justified war? Could any good be said to have come out of the largest and deadliest conflict in history?

1938

Hitler annexes Austria and begins the part occupation of Czechoslovakia.

1938

Britain and Germany sign a non-aggression pact.

TOTAL WAR

NAME: ADOLF HITLER

LIVED: 1889–1945

JOB: GERMAN FÜHRER

A soldier in World War I, Hitler became leader of the Nazi Party in 1921 and of Germany in 1934. He was driven by an overwhelming desire to overturn the Versailles Treaty, to create Lebensraum ('living room') for the growing population of Germany, and to destroy Europe's Jews. Hitler's ambitions drew the world into its deadliest conflict.

What led to the most widespread war in history, a conflict in which nations across the world used all their industrial, economic and technological might to wage 'total war'?

A HARSH PEACE

The road to war began when the German Chancellor Adolf Hitler began aggressively expanding German territory in the late 1930s. Germany's defeat in World War I had led to the harsh terms of the Treaty of Versailles. This reduced the country's territories and military, and forced it to pay huge reparations. The National Socialist Germany Workers (Nazi) party, led by Hitler, considered these terms humiliating. Economic depression and high unemployment in the 1920s boosted Nazi support as the party promised to restore national pride and create jobs. In 1934, Hitler became 'Führer' (leader) of the German Reich (state). Banning other political parties, he took total control of the country, pushing out and even killing those he thought 'undesirable', such as Jews and other minorities.

> "A BRITISH PRIME MINISTER HAS RETURNED FROM GERMANY BRINGING PEACE WITH HONOUR. I BELIEVE IT IS PEACE FOR OUR TIME."
>
> British Prime Minister Neville Chamberlain, 30 September 1938.

In Poland, the Royal Warsaw Castle burns after the Nazi invasion of 1939.

1939

September
Germany invades Poland. Britain and France declare war on Germany.

November
The Soviet Union invades Finland and occupies the Baltic States the following year.

1940

April
Germany invades and overruns Denmark and Norway.

Between 1 September and 6 October, 1939, German forces in the west and Soviet forces in the east invaded and occupied Poland, dividing the territory between them and signalling the start of World War II.

GERMANY

POLAND

SOVIET UNION

FAILED NEGOTIATIONS

In 1938, Hitler signed a non-aggression pact with British prime minister Neville Chamberlain (below left), stating his desire never to go to war with Britain again. On his return from Munich, the PM appeared in front of jubilant crowds. However, a year after the document was signed, German forces invaded Poland and Europe was plunged into its second war in less than 30 years.

British Prime Minister Neville Chamberlain meets with Adolf Hitler in Munich, in 1938, but fails to prevent the rush to war.

WORLD WAR II FIGURES

NAME: WINSTON CHURCHILL
LIVED: 1874–1965
JOB: BRITAIN'S WARTIME LEADER

Having been in the political wilderness before war was decared, Winston Churchill became prime minister in 1940. He inspired the population with his rousing, defiant radio broadcasts, leading the country to victory in 1945.

May

German forces advance into Holland, Belgium and France, forcing the evacuation of 320,000 men from Dunkirk.

June

Italy under Mussolini declares war against Britain and France. France surrenders to the Germans.

September

Hitler launches the Blitz against British cities. It lasts until May 1941, killing around 40,000 civilians.

GLOBAL CONFLICT

By October 1939, Poland had collapsed. Over the next three years, the conflict expanded to all parts of the globe. At first, there was a period of comparative peace, known as the 'phony war'. However, this quickly disappeared as war spread through Europe, Russia and the Pacific.

Key

■ Axis powers
■ Allied powers

WORLD WAR II FIGURES

★ ★

NAME: EMPEROR HIROHITO

LIVED: 1901–1989

JOB: EMPEROR OF JAPAN

Regarded as a living god by many Japanese before the war, the emperor was almost tried as a war criminal after it. In the end, he was allowed to keep his position but renounced his divinity.

A GROWING WAR

The war escalated quickly from April 1940 onwards as German forces overcame Denmark and Norway, followed by the Netherlands, Belgium and France. North Africa became a new theatre of conflict when the Italians came into the war and attacked British-controlled Egypt.
In 1941, Germany broke its non-aggression pact with the Soviet Union and invaded. At the end of the year, Germany's ally Japan attacked the US fleet at Pearl Harbor in Hawaii, bringing the United States into the war.

Battleships blaze and sink after the Japanese attack on Pearl Harbor.

1940

1941

September

Italy attacks British-controlled Egypt while British troops advance into Italian-controlled Libya.

April

German General Rommel attacks British forces in North Africa. The Allies capture Addis Ababa in Ethiopia from the Italians.

June

A huge German army of 3 million men invades the Soviet Union.

> "NOW THE ROUGH WORK HAS BEEN DONE WE BEGIN THE PERIOD OF FINER WORK. WE NEED TO WORK IN HARMONY WITH THE CIVIL ADMINISTRATION. WE COUNT ON YOU GENTLEMEN AS FAR AS THE FINAL SOLUTION IS CONCERNED."

Nazi leader Reinhard Heydrich addressing Nazi officials on the planned mass murder of all European Jews, 20 January 1942.

★ WORLD WAR II FIGURES ★

NAME: **FRANKLIN D. ROOSEVELT**

LIVED: **1882–1945**

JOB: **PRESIDENT OF THE UNITED STATES**

Although Roosevelt ensured that aid was supplied to Britain, the US remained neutral until the Japanese attack on Pearl Harbor. He then led his country to the brink of victory, dying of a stroke just before the end of the war.

MASS MURDER

The Nazis believed the Germans were a 'master race' and wanted to remove 'weaker' races, and particularly Jews, from society. After the invasion of Poland, separate areas, called ghettos, were set up for the Jewish population. As Germany marched into the Baltic states and the western Soviet Union in 1941, some 5 million Jews came under its control. In the same year, Hitler ordered the killing of all Jews. This 'Final Solution' to the Jewish 'problem' led to the creation of extermination camps across Europe, such as Auschwitz in Poland (above). Some 6 million Jews were transported to, and killed in, these camps, often in gas chambers, along with prisoners-of-war, political opponents, people with disabilities and minority groups.

The Mitsubishi 'Zero' was the main Japanese fighter aircraft in the war.

September

After huge gains, the German advance is stopped by the Soviet defence of Stalingrad. German armies reach Moscow the next month but are stopped by the Russian winter.

December

After the Japanese attack on the US Navy at Pearl Harbor, the USA declares war on Japan. Over the next few months, Japan swiftly overruns large parts of Southeast Asia.

THE END GAME

After nearly six years of brutal conflict, Germany and Japan were defeated within a few months of each other. But victory came at a terrible cost with bombing campaigns and the first use of nuclear weapons causing millions of civilian deaths.

Allied advance through France

GERMANY

Soviet advance

Allied advance through Italy

THE BATTLE FOR EUROPE

Until mid 1943, it could be claimed that Germany (and its allies) was winning the war. It had successfully invaded Romania, Greece and Yugoslavia, and brought Hungary into the conflict on its side. Furthermore, its Soviet campaign had started well with German troops pushing deep into Russian territory. From this point on, however, Germany would suffer a series of reverses that would lead to its defeat.

The Allied victory in North Africa in May 1943 and subsequent invasion of Italy forced Germany's main European ally out of the war. The Soviets then turned the tide in the east with victories at Stalingrad and Kursk causing the Germans to retreat. The D-Day landings in France in 1944 also brought a German retreat in the west. Soviet troops reached Berlin in May 1945, forcing Hitler's suicide and the defeat of Germany.

1942

1943

May/June

The USA defeats the Japanese navy at the battles of Coral Sea and Midway.

February

The German sixth army in Stalingrad surrenders. The defeat marks the end of Germany's advance into Russia and a major turning point in the war.

The Japanese battle cruiser *Mikumai* is sunk by US bombers during the Battle of Midway.

May

Following the surrender of the Axis forces in Tunisia, the Allies now control the whole of the North African coast.

July

Allied troops conquer Sicily and Mussolini is forced to resign.

The T-34 was the Soviet Union's main tank during the conflict.

WAR IN THE PACIFIC

The USA and Japan fought a series of naval battles in 1942 culminating in Japan's defeat at the Battle of Midway in June. US troops then began forcing the Japanese out of islands in the south Pacific seized earlier in the conflict. By early 1945, most of the Japanese conquests had been retaken and the bombing of Japan's cities began. Finally, in August, the US dropped two nuclear bombs on the cities of Hiroshima and Nagasaki. Japan surrendered a few days later.

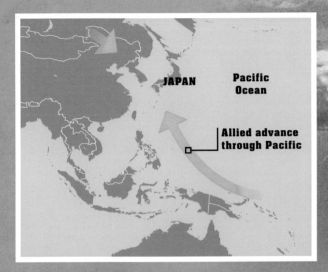

JAPAN

Pacific Ocean

Allied advance through Pacific

A mushroom cloud of dust and debris rises 6 km (3.5 miles) above the city of Hiroshima.

1944   1945

June

The Allies enter Rome on 4 June. On 6 June, the Allied army lands on the beaches of Normandy to begin the D-Day invasion of France.

March

The Allies enter Germany and link up with the Soviet Army. Facing defeat, Hitler commits suicide in his bunker in April.

May

The Allies accept Germany's surrender and declare Victory in Europe (VE Day).

August

The USA drops atomic bombs on the Japanese cities of Hiroshima and Nagasaki, prompting Japan's surrender.

US troops land on the Normandy beaches during D-Day.

AFTERMATH OF WAR

Following the German surrender, the leaders of the Soviet Union, the United States and Britain met at the Potsdam Conference in July and August 1945. There, the leaders agreed on the terms of Germany's surrender and its division into four Allied occupation zones (see map).

PHYSICAL DAMAGE

World War II saw unprecedented military casualties. But unlike World War I, the physical destruction extended far beyond the battlefield. Some 30 per cent of Great Britain's houses were destroyed or damaged. In France, Belgium and the Netherlands, the figure was around 20 per cent, while Germany saw the obliteration of 39 per cent of its dwellings. In the Far East, Japanese occupation led to substantial destruction in the Philippines, Burma and parts of China. Around 30 per cent of Japan's urban population lost their homes and Nagasaki and Hiroshima suffered the lasting damage of a nuclear explosion and radiation. Millions were made homeless, with an estimated 21 million refugees in Europe alone following the war. The result was human misery, suffering and deprivation on a vast scale.

Ruined buildings in the German city of Dresden.

CASUALTIES OF WAR

The total number of deaths caused by World War II can only be approximated. It is estimated at anything from 35 to 65 million, with twice as many civilians killed as soldiers. The heaviest proportion of deaths occurred in Eastern Europe: Poland lost around 20 per cent (5,800,000) of its population, the Soviet Union (18 million) and Yugoslavia (1.5 million) around 10 per cent of their populations and Germany (at 4,200,000) just under that. Unknown millions in China died during World War II as a result of Japanese occupation, famine, economic collapse and civil unrest.

POLAND

Key

Britain   USA

France   Returned
to other
USSR   countries

A ship burns off the coast
of Israel during the first
Arab-Israeli War in 1948.

PEACE AND CONFLICT

The final agreement of the Potsdam Conference acknowledged
Soviet dominance in Eastern Europe. In the same year, the United
Nations was established with 50 member nations signing up
to its goal: to work for peace, security and cooperation among
the nations of the world. In 1947, UN leaders voted that Palestine
should be divided into a Jewish state and an Arab state, with
Jerusalem under UN control. The Arab states, however,
rejected partition and the newly formed Israeli
government declared an independent state
of Israel. Arab-Israeli wars continued
over the following decades and
conflict in the region goes
on to this day.

A JUST WAR?

The overthrow of the Nazis, who were responsible for some of the worst examples of inhumanity in history, was the one clear positive to come out of the war. For many, the war was a fight against evil, making it justifiable and absolutely necessary. And yet the war was the deadliest and most destructive ever fought. Millions across the world lost their lives, cities were shattered, economies paralysed, and families were torn apart. For the millions who lost everything or grieved for their dead, was this a sacrifice worth making?

"... LIVING VISIONS OF HELL, PACKED WITH STARVING, DEHYDRATED, DISEASE-RIDDEN PRISONERS."

Descriptions of German concentration camps by US and British liberators, 1945.

Polish prisoners celebrate being liberated from Dachau concentration camp in Germany, 1945.

CONCENTRATION CAMPS

During the spring of 1945, Allied armies liberated concentration camps in Germany and eastern Europe, to which many inmates had been force-marched from other slave labour and extermination camps. The scenes the liberators witnessed were horrifying, with starving, disease-ridden prisoners living in appalling conditions alongside piles of unburied corpses.

CULTURAL CONFLICT

This giant statue, known as 'The Motherland Calls' was erected in 1967 to commemorate the Battle of Stalingrad.

The war fought on the Eastern Front, between the Soviet Union and Nazi Germany and their allies, caused enormous destruction and massive loss of life. Both Adolf Hitler and the Soviet leader Joseph Stalin showed a disregard for human life in their drive for victory, subjecting their own people to extreme brutality.
The conflict was known to the Soviets as the Great Patriotic War, a victory for Stalin and the Red Army. For other nations, the war was viewed differently. To the British, it was a fight against tyranny; to the Americans it was a war that saved democracy. The Japanese saw it as an opportunity to gain territory, while for the world's Jewish population it will always be associated with the Holocaust and the mass murder of 6 million Jews.

A Soviet officer urges on his troops to attack German invaders.

★ THE NUREMBURG TRIALS ★

From November 1945, 21 leading Nazis were put on trial at an international tribunal in Nuremberg, charged with violating the laws and customs of war, and crimes against humanity. As a result, 10 prisoners were executed, two committed suicide, while others were imprisoned. Many other Nazi war criminals, however, escaped punishment. The tribunal had a great influence on the development of international criminal law. It established the principle that individuals, and not just states, could be guilty of war crimes and that only by punishing individuals who commit such crimes can international law be enforced.

15

PEACE AGREEMENTS

An end to armed combat didn't mean an end to hostilities. Leaders from the victorious Allies met to discuss the terms of the peace. Although agreements were signed, relations between the capitalist west and the communist east became increasingly strained.

WARTIME MEETINGS

Even before the war ended, leaders from the key Allied nations, USA, Great Britain and the Soviet Union, met to discuss peace terms and post-war relations. This occurred first in February in Yalta in 1945 where it was agreed that Germany would be divided into four zones under the control of Britain, France, the Soviet Union and the USA. Berlin, which was in the Russian zone, would also be divided into four. It was also agreed that German war criminals would be punished and countries in East Europe would hold free elections for new governments.

GREAT BRITAIN

FRANCE

SWITZERLAND

WORLD WAR II FIGURES

NAME: **JOSEPH STALIN**

LIVED: **1878–1953**

JOB: **LEADER OF THE USSR**

A ruthless ruler who imprisoned and executed millions of his political 'enemies', Stalin led the Soviet Union to victory in World War II. Afterwards, he oversaw the country's development of nuclear weapons and emergence as a global superpower and chief rival to the USA.

The Allied leaders, Churchill, Roosevelt and Stalin meet at the Yalta Conference.

16

USSR

EAST GERMANY

POLAND

WEST GERMANY

CZECHOSLOVAKIA

AUSTRIA

HUNGARY

ROMANIA

YUGOSLAVIA

ITALY

BULGARIA

ALBANIA

GREECE

Key
Western bloc
Eastern bloc

THE DIVISION OF EUROPE

In July–August 1945, Stalin, Truman (who had succeeded Roosevelt as US president) and Churchill (who lost the British General Election during the conference and was replaced by Clement Attlee) met at the Potsdam Conference. Although they made some formal agreements, it was clear that the final division between east and west in Europe would be decided largely on where Soviet and American/British armies had met at the end of the war with Soviet forces occupying all the Eastern European countries.

With Britain and France seriously weakened by the war, the USA and the Soviet Union dominated world politics. Each country viewed the other with increasing suspicion and fear. Truman was worried by Stalin's communist influence in Eastern Europe and Stalin was concerned by Truman's 'powerful new weapon' deployed at the end of the war, the atomic bomb.

This sign marked the border between the Allied controlled zones in Berlin.

YOU ARE LEAVING THE AMERICAN SECTOR
ВЫ ВЫЕЗЖАЕТЕ ИЗ АМЕРИКАНСКОГО СЕКТОРА
VOUS SORTEZ DU SECTEUR AMÉRICAIN
SIE VERLASSEN DEN AMERIKANISCHEN SEKTOR
US ARMY

NEUE ZEIT UNION-VERLAG (VGB)

Between 1961 and 1989, a wall divided the capitalist western side from the communist eastern side of Berlin.

THE COLD WAR

Tension between the USA and the Soviet Union increased after the war as the two countries built up their armed forces, made threats to each other and formed opposing alliances. By 1948, most Eastern European countries had Communist governments controlled by Moscow. President Truman, fearing the further spread of Soviet power and communism, had set up the Marshall Plan, providing economic assistance to non-communist European countries.

MILITARY STAND-OFF

Relations worsened during the post-war years, leading Western Europe and the USA to form the military alliance of NATO. In response, the Soviet Union formed its own military alliance in 1955 with the communist countries of Eastern Europe, known as the Warsaw Pact. These two super alliances faced each other in a political and military stand-off that became known as the 'Cold War'.

US planes deliver much-needed supplies to West Berlin between 1 April 1948 and 12 May 1949, when the Soviet Union blocked land routes into the city in an unsuccessful attempt to drive the Allies out.

$372 NORWAY

$3,297 UNITED KINGDOM

$385 DENMARK

$1,128 NETHERLANDS

$133 IRELAND

$777 BELGIUM

$2,295 FRANCE

$205 SWITZERLAND

$70 PORTUGAL

This map shows the amount each nation received under the Marshall Plan in millions of US dollars.

★ THE MARSHALL PLAN ★

Whatever the weather We must move **together**

From 1948 to 1952, the US provided economic aid to the tune of US$13 billion to much of Western Europe. Known as the Marshall Plan, this helped Western Europe to recover from the war. Industrial and agricultural production got back on track fairly rapidly and standards of living improved dramatically over the next two decades. The plan also formed the basis of the European Economic Union.

A US fighter plane intercepts a
Soviet bomber in the early 1970s
at the height of the Cold War.

THE NUCLEAR THREAT

On 6 August and 9 August 1945, the
USA dropped atomic bombs on Japan
at Hiroshima and Nagasaki. Four years
later, the Soviets had developed nuclear
weapons of their own. The two sides
built vast nuclear arsenals that were
capable of destroying the world several
times over. This prevented them from
going to war with each other. Instead,
they competed using other means:
through propaganda, spying and by
supporting opposite sides in other
conflicts. This Cold War dominated
world politics for decades, through to
the break-up of the Soviet Union in
1991, and continues to affect world
politics today.

$1,448
WEST GERMANY

$468
AUSTRIA

$1,204
ITALY

$376
GREECE

$137
TURKEY

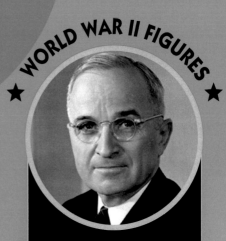

WORLD WAR II FIGURES

★   ★

NAME: HARRY S TRUMAN
LIVED: 1884–1972
JOB: PRESIDENT OF THE USA

When President Roosevelt died
suddenly in April 1945, his
vice president, Harry S
Truman, inherited the top job
and saw the USA through to
victory. He approved the use
of the atomic bombs that
ended the conflict. His period
in office (1945–1953) was
marked by an economic
boom in the US and by rising
tensions with the Soviet Union
that signalled the start of the
Cold War.

"THE ATOMIC BOMB IS TOO DANGEROUS TO BE LOOSE
IN A LAW-LESS WORLD. THAT IS WHY GREAT BRITAIN, CANADA
AND THE UNITED STATES, WHO HAVE THE SECRET OF ITS
PRODUCTION, DO NOT INTEND TO REVEAL THAT SECRET…"

President Truman, US radio broadcast on the Potsdam Conference, 9 August 1945.

INTERNATIONAL COOPERATION

The United Nations (UN) was officially established on 24 October 1945. Today, 191 nations are members, and its main goals are to maintain international peace and security, and to improve the lives of people around the world.

THE UNITED NATIONS

The UN tries to make sure people are treated equally regardless of race, gender, language and religion and meets regularly to discuss human rights issues. It also works to find peaceful solutions when there are disputes between nations and has also sent peacekeeping troops to trouble spots around the world, such as Somalia and Bosnia in 1992 and Afghanistan in 2002. The United Nations has also provided aid to thousands of refugees around the world as well as economic assistance to countries facing difficulties after a war.

The United Nations meets at the organisation's headquarters in New York City, USA.

"TO SAVE SUCCEEDING GENERATIONS FROM THE SCOURGE OF WAR... TO REAFFIRM FAITH IN FUNDAMENTAL HUMAN RIGHTS... TO ESTABLISH CONDITIONS UNDER WHICH JUSTICE AND RESPECT FOR THE OBLIGATIONS ARISING FROM TREATIES AND OTHER SOURCES OF INTERNATIONAL LAW CAN BE MAINTAINED, AND TO PROMOTE SOCIAL PROGRESS AND BETTER STANDARDS OF LIFE IN LARGER FREEDOM."

The UN Charter.

★ PARTITION OF INDIA ★

India was granted independence from Britain in 1947 but its partition into India and Pakistan (and subsequently Bangladesh) led to the deaths and displacement of hundreds of thousands of people.

WEST PAKISTAN

EAST PAKISTAN

INDIA

THE END OF EMPIRES

The world's two major imperial powers, Britain and France were severely weakened by the war. Over the next three decades, the majority of their overseas colonies gained independence. In Africa, national borders created by the European empires often left newly independent countries divided and ruled by increasingly corrupt governments. France fought long, drawn-out wars to preserve its colonies, in particular in Algeria and Vietnam.

PEACE PROBLEMS

Despite its best intentions, the United Nations has often had considerable difficulties achieving its goals. During the Cold War, the organisation was often made to look ineffective by the superpowers. Both the Soviet Union and the US regularly blocked any resolutions that might harm their interests or those of their allies.

Protestors barricade the streets during the Algerian War of Independence in 1960.

ECONOMIC CHANGE

In Britain and the US, many women worked in factories for the first time during World War II, and they changed the face of industry when they demanded the right to carry on working after the war was over.

The physical destruction of World War II had severe repercussions for economies around the world. Across Europe, homes, schools, hospitals, factories, transport systems and more had been destroyed and would need to be rebuilt so that nations could thrive again.

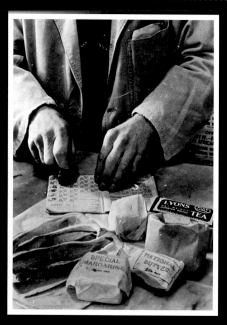

A shopkeeper stamps a ration book in Britain during the war.

SHORTAGES AND HARDSHIP

In Nazi-occupied territories throughout Europe, most particularly in Eastern Europe, resources were ruthlessly exploited with workers relocated to perform forced labour for German needs. Transport systems were completely disrupted and agriculture suffered due to a lack of workers, machinery and fertilisers. As a result, the economies of much of Europe suffered greatly after 1945.

SOVIET SURVIVAL

The Soviet Union, which had seen the biggest loss of life during the war, also saw its economy virtually crippled. Yet it still had a big and powerful army and access to extensive resources, including machinery and raw materials from Soviet-occupied Eastern Europe. This enabled it to recover after the war and retain its status as a military superpower.

YOUR VICTORY GARDEN
counts more than ever!

US poster encouraging people to grow their own vegetables to help overcome the wartime food shortages.

★ REFUGEES ★

Across the world, many millions of people were made homeless as a result of the war, and by the end of the war, Europe had around 40 million refugees. Many women suffered extreme sexual violence. During the later stages of the war, the Red Army soldiers committed mass rape against more than a million young women as they advanced into German territories; and as many as 200,000 women (known as comfort women) were forced into sexual slavery by the Japanese army.

ECONOMIC POWER AND RECOVERY

In the USA, many Americans actually benefited from World War II. Increased war production in the USA had led to an industrial boom, which raised living standards and brought in an era of US global market domination. By 1945, the USA was the world's greatest military and economic power. It was also able to help the recovery of the defeated nations. Marshall Plan loans helped to rebuild Germany's economy in the 1950s. Japan, meanwhile, which the USA occupied until 1952, underwent a post-war 'economic miracle'. By the 1980s, it had become the world's second largest economy after the United States.

The post-war recovery of Japanese industry meant that innovative luxury goods produced in Japan, such as transistor radios (invented in the 1940s), were soon in demand all over the world.

THE RISE OF STATE CONTROL

On both sides of the Atlantic during the war, governments controlled the supply of food and supplies to the population, although rationing was not as intense in the US as it was in Britain.

In the US and Britain, food, fuel and clothing were rationed during and after the war years.

SOCIAL REVOLUTION

After the war, Great Britain suffered from huge post-war debt and a shortage of food supplies and raw materials. As a result, rationing of food, clothing and other goods survived right through to 1954. The upheaval of war had a vast impact on the mood of the country, The sufferings of the Blitz, ration books and identity cards created a sense of equality in sacrifice and togetherness. Large sections of the population, who had previously been separated from one another, were now thrown together.

Rosie the Riveter featured in a US government propaganda campaign to boost public morale and to encourage women to take on jobs usually done by men.

"THERE IS NO FINER INVESTMENT FOR ANY COMMUNITY THAN PUTTING MILK INTO BABIES."

Winston Churchill, radio broadcast, 21 March 1943. During World War II, the government introduced free school meals and milk.

FROM CRADLE TO GRAVE

The feelings of unity and equality that the war effort inspired, along with increased government control during the conflict, led to a new faith in social planning and public policy. Published in 1942, the Beveridge Report summed up this new mood. It proposed a post-war scheme of social security, providing child allowances and maternity benefits, old age pensions and unemployment benefits to look after people from 'the cradle to the grave'. It proved hugely popular with the British people.

William Beveridge, the author of the report that became the basis of Britain's Welfare State.

LABOUR LANDSLIDE

Although Churchill was considered a great war time leader, his political party did not support the Beveridge Report. In 1945, this led to a surprise landslide victory for his opponents, the Labour party, who did. The Labour government started six years of reform, creating a state based on a mixed economy and welfare, which remained in place until the 1980s.

The Labour leader, Clement Attlee who followed Churchill as Prime Minister in 1945.

NATIONAL HEALTH

The new Labour government took around 20 per cent of the country's major industries into public ownership and extended the welfare state. This involved creating a National Health Service in 1948 which, for the first time, provided free medical care for all citizens. The National Health Service still forms a key part of the UK government policy today.

THE NEW
NATIONAL HEALTH SERVICE

Your new National Health Service begins on 5th July. What is it? How do you get it?

It will provide you with all medical, dental, and nursing care. Everyone—rich or poor, man, woman or child—can use it or any part of it. There are no charges, except for a few special items. There are no insurance qualifications. But it is not a "charity". You are all paying for it, mainly as taxpayers, and it will relieve your money worries in time of illness.

WEAPONS OF WAR

Technology and science had a crucial role in deciding the outcome of World War II. Scientists, mathematicians and specialists in a number of fields were given huge resources to work on the development of new initiatives that might make a difference to the conflict. The war saw huge advances in the fields of science, technology, mathematics and medicine, all of which have had a major effect on our lives today.

A German Messerschmitt Me 262, the first operational jet fighter.

★ AIRCRAFT

Aircraft underwent rapid advances during the war, as pilots fought for air superiority and engineers tried to develop the ultimate air weapon. Innovations included the building of large, long-range bomber aircraft, such as the B-29 Superfortress which was used by the USA against Japan. Jet engines were also introduced, first by the Germans and later by the British. Jet aircraft are now used by military air forces and commercial airlines worldwide.

★ RADAR

Radar technology improved in the war. The ability to use radio waves to detect objects at a distance made 'surprise attacks' less likely. Radar stations, such as the one below, allowed combatants to track incoming air attacks, guide fighter aircraft to their targets and direct anti-aircraft guns towards enemy airplanes. Radar signals could also be used for navigation and the technology set the foundation for many modern electronics.

A British soldier carrying a machine gun.

A US army Jeep.

★WEAPONRY AND SMALL ARMS

More powerful anti-aircraft and anti-tank weapons were developed in the war and the use of light, portable machine guns also spread. The USA issued its troops with the first semi-automatic (or self-loading) rifles, which gave them a major advantage over German troops still using old-fashioned, manually loaded rifles.

★ VEHICLES

Tanks, which had been developed in World War I continued to see advances in firepower, armour and speed. The US Army also introduced a new general purpose vehicle, the Jeep, which proved hugely successful both during and after the war. Amphibious vehicles, which could transport troops and supplies across water and land, and which were used in the D-Day landings, were also developed for the war.

★ ROCKETS

Military scientists also put considerable resources into developing rockets and flying bombs. The Germans came up with the V-1 flying bomb and the V-2 rocket, which were used to attack Allied targets from 1944. The V-2 acted as the forerunner to both modern long-range missiles and space rockets. The scientists who developed these weapons for Germany were moved to the US and USSR after the war where they helped to build the rockets that sent astronauts into space and to the Moon.

WORLD WAR II FIGURES

NAME: WERNHER VON BRAUN

LIVED: 1912–1977

JOB: ROCKET SCIENTIST

A brilliant German scientist, von Braun was employed by the Nazis to develop their V2 rocket. Wanting to make use of his talents, the US smuggled him out of Germany after the war. He went on to design the Saturn V rocket that sent the first men to the Moon in 1969.

Thousands of V-2s were launched against London, Antwerp and other targets towards the end of the war, causing widespread destruction and loss of life.

CODE-BREAKERS

NAME: ALAN TURING

LIVED: 1912–1954

JOB: CODE-BREAKER

English mathematician Alan Turing was the key figure behind Bletchley Park's Bombe machine that helped decoders read German messages encrypted by the Enigma machine. After the war, he worked on blueprints for a digital computer and undertook important research into artificial intelligence. In 1952, he was arrested and tried for homosexuality, then a criminal offence. He committed suicide on 7 June 1954. In 2009, the British government issued an apology for the way he was treated and in 2013 he was given a posthumous pardon by Queen Elizabeth II.

In early 1940, mathematicians at Bletchley Park in England cracked Enigma, a complex cipher (secret writing) machine used by the Germans to communicate classified military information. The code-breakers were aided by high-speed electro-mechanical devices known as Bombes, the forerunner to today's computers.

A German navy Enigma machine, which used a combination of dials to produce coded messages.

HELPING THE WAR EFFORT

The secret intelligence passed on by Bletchley Park – codenamed 'Ultra' – to the British government played a crucial role in the Allied victory, saving millions of lives. Intercepted, decoded enemy messages, along with advances in radar, helped the British route ships away from German U-boats during the Battle of the Atlantic. The intelligence also contributed to Allied victories in Italy, North Africa (where the Royal Navy was able to cut German supply lines) and in the D-Day landings, helping to confuse Hitler over where the Allies were to land.

FIRST ELECTRONIC COMPUTER

The Colossus, the world's first working electronic computer, was also developed at Bletchley Park. It was invented by British engineer Tommy Flowers to speed up the breaking of another even more complex German cipher machine used by Hitler and his generals, known as the Lorenz. Colossus machines were destroyed at the end of the war and remained classified information until 1975. However, the knowledge that high-speed electronic digital computer machines were possible certainly had an influence on the development of early computers in the UK and US.

An operator inputs instructions into the Colossus computer at Bletchley Park in 1943.

"THE INTELLIGENCE... FROM YOU [BLETCHLEY PARK]... HAS BEEN OF PRICELESS VALUE. IT HAS SAVED THOUSANDS OF BRITISH AND AMERICAN LIVES AND, IN NO SMALL WAY, CONTRIBUTED TO THE SPEED WITH WHICH THE ENEMY WAS ROUTED AND EVENTUALLY FORCED TO SURRENDER."

General Dwight D Eisenhower, US president (1953–1961).

Bletchley Park in England where British intelligence officers cracked the Enigma code in World War II.

THE ATOMIC BOMB

Between 1942 and 1946, the United States mobilised a huge number of scientists and engineers as part of the secret Manhattan Project with the aim of developing the first atomic bombs. The project was a success; the devices dropped on Hiroshima and Nagasaki ended the war and signalled the start of the Nuclear Age.

THE ARMS RACE

The atomic bomb was the biggest military development of the war, with far-reaching implications for international politics, society and our lives today. For the first time, one weapon carried by a single aircraft could destroy an entire city.

The Soviet Union developed nuclear weapons in 1949 and nuclear competition between the two superpowers would be a large part of the Cold War. Several other countries around the world also developed their own weapons. In recent decades, leaders of countries that have these weapons agreed to limit their production, testing and use. More recently, there have been concerns about the threat of nuclear or biological attacks by terrorist groups.

These ruins from the nuclear blast in Hiroshima now form part of a memorial to the conflict.

A Russian intercontinental nuclear weapon mounted on a truck.

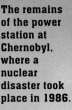

CONCERNS AND BENEFITS

Nuclear energy is not just present in bombs. It is also used to create electricity, and to power submarines and other naval vessels. It also has a medical role. Doctors use radioactive elements to locate tumours and other diseases in the body, and treat cancer patients with controlled radiation. Supporters of nuclear energy argue that it is a safe, sustainable energy and that its greenhouse gas emissions are far smaller than the burning of coal, oil and gas. It is also argued that the existence of nuclear weapons has made the world a safer place, making conventional war less likely.

But the radiation caused by nuclear energy can be extremely harmful to humans, animals and plants, causing cancers and genetic damage. One of the worst nuclear power plant accidents happened in 1986 in Chernobyl in the western Soviet Union after a nuclear reactor exploded. Harmful gases leaked out and spread across Europe, contaminating crops and livestock, and causing deadly cancers in hundreds of people. Another issue of concern is the safe disposal of nuclear waste. The risk of radiation leaks and catastrophic accidents has led to great public opposition to nuclear power.

The remains of the power station at Chernobyl, where a nuclear disaster took place in 1986.

31

MEDICINE

World War II produced advances in medicine, innovating, improving and further refining developments made in the pre-war years.

★ FOOD NUTRITION

In order to ensure their soldiers were fighting fit, US scientists conducted in-depth research into food nutrition, identifying which vitamins and minerals were essential for optimum health. Soldiers' ration packs (see left) were then carefully formulated and the storage, handling and preparation of food became a top priority for the military during the conflict.

★ FIGHTING MALARIA

As the conflict spread to the Pacific where mosquito-borne malaria was a threat, American servicemen were given an anti-malarial drug called atabrine. The insecticide DDT was also developed and sprayed over large areas to control outbreaks of malaria. DDT is still used as an agricultural pesticide spray in many parts of the world, although concerns over its deadly impact on wildlife has led to it being banned in the US.

NAZI RESEARCH

During the war, the Nazis carried out many forced medical experiments on prisoners in concentration camps. Performed mainly on Jews, these experiments often involved deliberately causing serious injuries or infecting patients with diseases in order to test possible treaments. Many of the doctors responsible for the experiments were put on trial at Nuremberg after the war and either imprisoned or executed.

These Men DIDN'T TAKE THEIR ATABRINE

KAZZ

This gruesome sign, erected in Papua New Guinea during the war, warns US soldiers to take their anti-malarial drugs.

★ PENICILLIN AND ANTIBIOTICS

While the antibiotic penicillin had already been discovered, companies during the war began producing it in much bigger quantities and making versions that were far stronger. British and US forces used penicillin to treat wounds, greatly reducing the chance of infection and improving survival rates. After the war, it was used to treat the once fatal disease of pneumonia. Penicillin is still in use today and was the precursor to many other types of antibiotic. However, the widespread overuse of antibiotics has also led to the increase in resistant bacteria, such as MRSA.

Antibiotics first became widely available in World War II, saving millions of lives.

★ BLOOD TRANSFUSIONS

The blood transfusion service – particularly the storing of blood and distributing it to where it is needed – was greatly improved during the war. Great advances were also made in tetanus immunisations, reconstructive surgery and the treatment of burns.

A soldier receives a blood tranfusion in an army hospital.

OTHER INNOVATIONS

A host of other innovations and inventions came out of the war, many of which have had a big effect on our day-to-day lives.

★ JERRYCANS

In the 1930s, the Germans designed and produced a tough steel container for carrying fuel. Solidly built and able to be used again and again, it was adopted and copied by American and British forces during the war, who called it the jerrycan (after the Allied slang term for Germans; 'jerry').

"WITHOUT THESE CANS IT WOULD HAVE BEEN IMPOSSIBLE FOR OUR ARMIES TO CUT THEIR WAY ACROSS FRANCE AT A LIGHTNING PACE WHICH EXCEEDED THE GERMAN BLITZKRIEG OF 1940."

US President Franklin D Roosevelt.

★ SYNTHETIC RUBBER

The Japanese occupation of most of Southeast Asia, where rubber is harvested from trees (see left), cut off the Allies' supplies of natural rubber. This led to a great expansion in the production of synthetic rubber, which is now used in industries throughout the world.

★ CABIN PRESSURE SYSTEMS

Flying at high altitudes puts pilots at risk from both the lack of oxygen and low pressures which can cause decompression sickness. Although aircrew were equipped with oxygen masks from the start of the war, in 1944, the first cabin pressure system was developed for the US bomber, the B29 Superfortress. This innovation is carried by all passenger planes today.

The cabin-pressure system allowed the B29 bomber to undertake long-range missions without risking the crew's health.

294106

★ SUBSTITUTE MATERIALS

With resources focused on the war effort, many basic items, such as rubber and paper, were in short supply – so new materials emerged to meet demand. The 1940s saw the mass-production of plastics for the first time. In the US, cardboard juice and milk containers replaced glass bottles, plastic wrap or cellophane was used as a substitute for foil, while plywood replaced metals.

★NYLON STOCKINGS

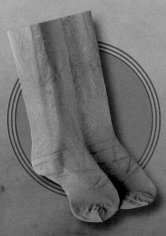

In the US, the creation of synthetic fibres in the 1930s led to the first nylon stockings being commercially produced in 1939. They sold 64 million pairs in the first year of production. By 1942, production of stockings ceased, as nylon was being used instead to make parachutes and tents. In the UK, nylon stockings were the favourite gift of American soldiers to impress British women, many of whom had never seen them before. Today, they are a common item of clothing across the world.

THE HOLOCAUST REMEMBERED

It is important that the memory of the Holocaust – the murder of 6 million Jews and other 'undesirables' – is kept alive to prevent such horrors from ever happening again. The terrible events are remembered in a number of ways including memorials, memoirs, novels and films.

THE HOLOCAUST IN LITERATURE

Holocaust survivors have written a wealth of literature, including the works of the Italian-Jewish chemist and author Primo Levi. His *If This Is a Man* (1947) tells of the year he spent as a prisoner at Auschwitz. More recently, the Holocaust has featured in *The Book Thief* (2005), a novel for young adults, written by Markus Zusak, in which the Holocaust is narrated by Death himself. *The Boy in the Striped Pyjamas* (2006) by John Boyne also presents the Holocaust from the perspective of a child. Both books were made into films.

Looking like a giant cemetery, The Memorial to the Murdered Jews of Europe was erected in Berlin in 2004.

★ WORLD WAR II FIGURES ★

NAME: **ANNE FRANK**

LIVED: **1929–1945**

JOB: **WRITER**

Dutch diarist and teenager Anne Frank wrote one of the most powerful accounts of Jewish life during World War II. Her diary tells of the two years she and her family spent hiding from the occupying Nazi army in a small annexe in Amsterdam from 1942. The family was discovered in 1944 and transported to Auschwitz and the prison camp Bergen-Belsen where Anne and her sister died. Her diary has since been translated into 60 languages and acts as a powerful reminder of the tragedy of the Holocaust.

ESCAPE TO HOLLYWOOD

Hitler's rise to power and occupation of much of Europe saw many German and Austrian writers, artists and film-makers fleeing to France, Britain and the USA to escape the Nazi regime.

FILMING THE HOLOCAUST

The Holocaust has been the subject of many films since the war, including *Night and Fog* (1955), *Sophie's Choice* (1982) and *Schindler's List* (1993). In Central and Eastern European countries, where the populations suffered most from the genocide, the Holocaust has been a particularly important theme in novels and films. The latter include the semi-documentary *The Last Stage* (1947) by Auschwitz survivor Wanda Jakubowska and *The Pianist* by Polish director Roman Polanksi.

★ WORLD WAR II FIGURES ★

NAME: **BILLY WILDER**

LIVED: **1906–2002**

JOB: **FILM DIRECTOR**

Some of the arrivals in the USA became famous and successful. These included Billy Wilder, an Austrian-born Jewish screenwriter. Following the rise of the Nazi party, Wilder moved from Berlin to Paris, and then to Hollywood in 1933. He became one of Hollywood's leading directors, creating classic films, such as *The Seven Year Itch* (1955) and *Some Like It Hot* (1959).

"ONE SINGLE ANNE FRANK MOVES US MORE THAN THE COUNTLESS OTHERS WHO SUFFERED JUST AS SHE DID BUT WHOSE FACES HAVE REMAINED IN THE SHADOWS. PERHAPS IT IS BETTER THAT WAY; IF WE WERE CAPABLE OF TAKING IN ALL THE SUFFERING OF ALL THOSE PEOPLE, WE WOULD NOT BE ABLE TO LIVE."

Author and Holocaust survivor Primo Levi.

CINEMA

In London, people queue up outside a cinema to watch a newsreel about the latest developments in the war.

Both sides understood the power of cinema. The Nazis commissioned propaganda films to spread their political messages. The British government thought that films might inspire dangerous thoughts in the audience and briefly banned cinema-going in 1939. The glamorous lives portrayed in US films often provided a distraction from the horrors of war.

INFORMING THE NATION

Cinema attendances grew steadily throughout the war, with between 25 and 35 million tickets sold every week in the UK alone. Films provided a way of instructing and entertaining the nation in wartime. Some of the many classic films of the period, such as *In Which We Serve* (1942), provided accounts of the nation's experience of war and were used to boost morale. With cheap ticket prices, people went to the cinema not only to watch films but also to see newsreels, cartoons or simply to keep warm, see friends or find comfort.

Shirley Temple was a child star in the 1930s, appearing in hit movies such as *Bright Eyes* (1934) and continuing as a cinema favourite throughout the war years.

ESCAPISM

What audiences really wanted was the glamour, escapism and movie stars provided by the Hollywood studios. By then the global centre of the film industry, Hollywood released some of its most memorable and best-loved films during the war years. These included *Gone with the Wind* (1939), probably the most popular film of the period, *The Wizard of Oz* (1939), *Rebecca* (1940), *Citizen Kane* (1941), *Casablanca* (1943) and *National Velvet* (1945).

POST-WAR CINEMA

After the war, cinema-going in the US briefly declined, largely as a result of the availability of television. From the late 1940s onwards, Hollywood was also rocked by the black-listing of more than 300 actors, writers and directors, who were accused of being communists. The tensions of the Cold War, and a growing fear of communism created a campaign by senior US government officials to try and drive out 'reds' from American life altogether.

The war proved a popular theme for film-makers, far more so than World War I, and even today the demand for films about World War II appears unstoppable. From *The Cruel Sea* (1953) and *Where Eagles Dare* (1968) to *Saving Private Ryan* (1998) and *The Imitation Game* (2014), audiences are still captivated by the war.

Poster for the 1942 film *Casablanca*, a romance about the resistance to the Nazis in North Africa.

> ## "WHAT AGENT OF CHANCELLOR HITLER IS IT WHO HAS SUGGESTED THAT WE SHOULD ALL COWER IN DARKNESS AND TERROR 'FOR THE DURATION'?"

British author George Bernard Shaw in *The Times*, 5 September 1939, in protest against the government order to close all places of entertainment in the UK.

Tora! Tora! Tora! (1970) was an American–Japanese war film that dramatized the Japanese attack on Pearl Harbor.

NEWS AND PROPAGANDA

Adolf Hitler and the Nazi Party made extensive use of propaganda – material and information produced to persuade people of a point of view. Their aim was to convince the German people of the rightness of their cause as well as to intimidate others into thinking that the political and military might of Nazi Germany was too great to be challenged.

Searchlights iluminate the sky at a mass rally for the Nazi Party in Nuremberg, 1937.

WORLD WAR II FIGURES

NAME: DR JOSEPH GOEBBELS

LIVED: 1897–1945

JOB: PROPAGANDA MINISTER

In his role as Minister of Propaganda, Goebbels organised the burning of 'un-German' books, commissioned antisemitic films and newspapers, and erected loudspeakers on the streets and distributed radios so everyone could hear Hitler's speeches. A devoted disciple of Hitler, he remained loyal to the leader to the end, committing suicide alongside him in the Berlin bunker.

> "THE ESSENCE OF PROPAGANDA CONSISTS IN WINNING PEOPLE OVER TO AN IDEA SO SINCERELY, SO VITALLY, THAT IN THE END THEY SUCCUMB TO IT UTTERLY AND CAN NEVER ESCAPE FROM IT."
>
> Dr Joseph Goebbels.

★ RALLYING SUPPORT

There were massive Nazi rallies in the 1930s designed to show the world the might of the Third Reich. In 1936, the Nazis also staged the Olympics in Berlin with the aim of showcasing the sporting superioity of the German race. But their plans were thwarted when the black American sprinter Jesse Owens won four gold medals.

Jesse Owens was the star of the Berlin Olympics.

★ CONTROLLING INFORMATION

With Dr Joseph Goebbels as head of propaganda, the Nazi Party controlled all forms of literature, art, music, radio, film and newspapers, and introduced a strict system of censorship, banning anything they did not agree with. Poster art and films produced by the Nazis promoted the need for total war, the greatness of Hitler and Germany and criticised Jewish people. Book burnings, such as this one in Berlin, saw millions of 'anti-Nazi' works, including those written by Jewish authors, destroyed.

★ SLOGANS FROM THE MINISTRY

We want your KITCHEN WASTE

PIG

The Allies also used propaganda. In the US, the Office of War Information, and in Britain, the Ministry of Information, used radio broadcasts, cinema newsreels (there was no TV) and newspapers to get their message across. They also issued advice to people, in the form of pamphlets and posters, such as the one on the left, on how to cope on limited rations, and how to save and recycle waste.

SERVICE ON THE HOME FRONT

★ CITIZENS DEFENSE CORPS
★ CITIZENS SERVICE CORPS
★ AMERICAN UNITY
★ SALVAGE PROGRAM
★ VICTORY GARDENS

Save waste fats for explosives

TAKE THEM TO YOUR MEAT DE

★ STIRRING SPEECHES

Radio was the chief source of news and entertainment, and listening increased during wartime. In the UK, Winston Churchill (left) and King George V frequently addressed the nation on the radio. In the US, a wide array of media, including radio, newspapers and movies, was used for propaganda purposes: to promote US involvement in the war, to encourage hatred of the enemy, and to drive war production.

★ CALLING THE WORLD ★

Britain's BBC World Service, or The Overseas Service, as it was called in 1939, launched 38 different language services during the war, providing opposition to Nazi rule in Europe. With Europe occupied, resistance leaders found their way to the BBC. The French general Charles de Gaulle broadcast from London in 1940. In 1945, as Allied troops moved through Europe, the true horrors of the Nazi concentration camps were also brought to light by the BBC. By 1945, the BBC was the biggest international broadcasting organisation in the world (as it still is today), broadcasting in 45 languages.

BBC

THE BIG QUESTIONS

It is difficult to consider anything good coming out of a massive human tragedy like World War II, and it is important to be clear how catastrophic the war was, how unimaginably high the human toll, and how far-reaching the consequences. For many people, World War Two had a clear moral purpose: it was a fight against the aggression of the Nazis. Once the grim realities of the Nazi death camps were revealed, the horror of Hitler's regime was there for all to see, and its overthrow was one clear 'good' of the Allied victory.

★ CIVILIAN CASUALTIES

World War II was the deadliest conflict ever fought, a 'total' war in which the full industrial, technological and economic might of nations were unleashed with devastating results. Unlike World War I, the graves of soldiers (such as these in Belgium) were outnumbered more than two to one by those of civilians. Between 35 and 65 million people lost their lives through genocide, mass-slaughter, starvation and deprivation, The desire for more powerful weaponry, as well as the huge increase in aerial bombing, culminated in the world's most dangerous and frightening weapon: the atomic bomb.

Firefighters try to put out a
blaze caused by German
bombs during the Blitz, 1941.

★ NEW NATIONS

After the war, the global empires of France and Great Britain began to break up. Over the next few decades, most of the imperial nations achieved independence – sometimes peacefully, sometimes through conflict – allowing the peoples there the chance to govern themselves. The process wasn't without problems. Several of the new nations endured civil wars and suffered corrupt governments. The establishment of a Jewish nation, Israel, in the wake of the Holocaust, continues to be a source of conflict in the region today.

....

ISRAEL
WEST BANK
GAZA

A map showing Israel (blue) and the Palestinian Territories (green). The flag of Israel is shown top left.

★ A DIVIDED WORLD

Out of the turmoil of war emerged shattered nations, with towns and cities destroyed, economies in tatters, families torn apart, and millions of refugees without homes or sustenance. The resulting peace agreements led to an immediate split between the capitalist west and the communist east. They remained hugely distrustful of each other for decades to come, with both sides building up huge stockpiles of long-range missiles capable of carrying nuclear warheads (such as this one). This 'Cold War' dominated world politics for the next 50 years. The risks of nuclear warfare and concerns over the safety of the nuclear industry are shadows under which we all still live.

"WAR IS NO LONGER MADE BY SIMPLY ANALYSED ECONOMIC FORCES, IF IT EVER WAS. WAR IS MADE OR PLANNED NOW BY INDIVIDUAL MEN, DEMAGOGUES AND DICTATORS WHO PLAY ON THE PATRIOTISM OF THEIR PEOPLE TO MISLEAD THEM INTO A BELIEF IN THE GREAT FALLACY OF WAR WHEN ALL THEIR VAUNTED REFORMS HAVE FAILED TO SATISFY THE PEOPLE THEY MISRULE."

Ernest Hemingway, *Notes on the Next War: A Serious Topical Letter* (1935).

POSITIVE EFFECTS OF WORLD WAR II

World War II saw such unprecedented death rates, destruction and misery that it's difficult to talk about 'positive' effects. How could anything positive come out of such carnage? But the war did bring about many beneficial changes: new commitments by governments to improve the lives of citzens; new technologies, initially devised for weapons but put to more peaceful purposes after the war; and new international bodies tasked with preventing a repeat of the conflict.

★ CARE OF THE STATE

Post-war governments introduced polices designed to make the lives of their poorer citizens better – partly to recognise how the sacrifices of the conflict had been endured by all members of society. They built new houses and introduced benefits for low-paid workers. In British hospitals (such as this one), free health care was offered as part of a National Health Service.

★ TECHNOLOGICAL ADVANCES

As in all wars, the drive to create better weapons also saw advances in other, less deadly technologies. World War II saw significant improvements in the fields of air travel (in the form of jet engines and improved radar), space exploration (the rocket technology used for German missiles would later send men to the Moon), computing (the world's first electronic computer, shown here, was invented to crack a German code) and medicine (in the form of improved antibiotics and other drugs).

★ ECONOMIC RECOVERY

The economies of many nations, including Britain and the Soviet Union were ravaged by the war. The USA, however, enjoyed an post-war industrial boom, when its citizens could afford luxuries, such as the latest motor cars (left). The desire not to repeat the mistakes of the World War I peace settlement led to the USA helping the defeated nations of Germany and Japan rebuild their economies.

★ INTERNATIONAL ORGANISATIONS

The catastrophic nature of the war, the loss of millions of lives and the immense physical destruction triggered changes in many fields. It changed the balance of power in the world, and led to the establishment of the United Nations (UN) in 1945, an organisation set up to help maintain international peace, security and cooperation. The following decades saw the UN widen its remit to include health and medicine (World Health Organisation), finance (World Bank), culture (UNESCO) and many other areas.

While the world is still plagued by greed, inequality, extremism and conflict, more people today live longer and have a far higher standard of living than ever before. Nor have we experienced a global conflict of such scale since 1945.

"WE HAVE DISCOVERED THAT THERE IS SOMETHING MORE HORRIBLE THAN WAR – THE KILLING OF THE SPIRIT IN THE BODY, THE NAZI CONTEMPT FOR THE INDIVIDUAL MAN. THE WORLD REEKS WITH THE FOULNESS OF THE CRIMES IN OCCUPIED EUROPE, WHERE A DARK AGE HAS BEGUN ANEW."

Editorial in the *Times Literary Supplement* 1941.

The flags of the member nations flutter outside the headquarters of the UN in New York.

GLOSSARY

armageddon
A conflict that could destroy the world.

antibiotics
A type of medicine that destroys or prevents the growth of bacterial infection.

Cold War
The tension and hostility that built up between Eastern powers (the Soviet Union and its allies) and Western countries (the USA and Western powers) from 1945 to 1990.

concentration camp
A place where people are held as prisoners for political reasons.

Eastern Front
The theatre of war fought between the Nazis and its allies against the Soviet Union, Poland and its allies in central, southern and eastern Europe.

Enigma
A secret writing machine used by the Germans to send important military information in code.

Final Solution
The Nazi policy for exterminating the Jewish population in German-occupied territories.

ghetto
A part of a city where minority groups, such as Jewish people, are forced to live.

Holocaust
The mass-murder of Jews under the German Nazi regime.

immunisation
A treatment that makes someone resistant to a disease.

jet engine
A very fast engine used to power some airplanes.

malaria
A disease caused by parasites and transmitted by infected mosquitoes in tropical areas of the world.

military intelligence
The collection of information that is of military or political value.

NATO (the North Atlantic Treaty Organization)
A military alliance formed by Western powers in North America and Europe as a result of the Cold War. Member states agreed to defend each other should any be attacked.

nuclear or atomic bomb
A powerful weapon that creates a huge explosion. The huge power of the bomb is created by releasing enormous amounts of energy from the central part of an atom.

radar
A system that sends out electromagnetic waves to detect the presence of objects, such as aircraft.

radiation
Energy that moves from one place to another. Nuclear radiation carries a lot of energy and can be very dangerous to people, animals and the environment.

refugee
A person who has been forced to leave their country to escape war or persecution.

reparations
Compensation paid by a defeated country to cover war damage.

total war
A war in which combatants use all their resources – economic, industrial or technological.

United Nations
An international organisation founded in 1945 to prevent another worldwide conflict and to promote cooperation, and peace.

Warsaw Pact
Formed during the Cold War, this was a defensive and military agreement between eight communist countries in Europe.

Welfare State
A system where the government provides assistance to the old, sick, disabled or unemployed.

FURTHER INFORMATION

★ BOOKS TO READ

The Diary of a Young Girl
Anne Frank
(Puffin, 2007)
In 1942, Anne Frank and her family were forced to go into hiding during the Nazi occupation of Amsterdam. Thirteen-year-old Anne vividly describes in her diary the horrors and frustrations of living in confinement.

History Year by Year
(Dorling Kindersley, 2013)
A definitive world history for children, from the time when humans first walked the Earth to the age of social media.

Oxford Children's History of the World
Neil Grant
(Oxford University Press, 2000)
An illustrated book on the whole of human history, beginning with ancient times and ending with the world today.

★ MUSEUMS AND WEBSITES TO VISIT

Bletchley Park
The Mansion
Bletchley Park
Sherwood Drive
Bletchley
Milton Keynes
MK3 6EB
www.bletchleypark.org.uk
Bletchley Park was the wartime centre of Britain's codebreaking operation. Visitors to the museum can see the codebreaking huts, where Alan Turing amongst others worked, as well as a working reconstruction of a Colossus computer.

Imperial War Museum London
Lambeth Road
London SE1 6HZ
www.iwm.org.uk/visits/iwm-london
Second World War Galleries tell moving stories from the war and from the Home Front.

www.bbc.co.uk/schools/primaryhistory/world_war2

www.ducksters.com/history/world_war_ii/

www.historylearningsite.co.uk/world-war-two/

INDEX